Senen Francois Xavier

Conciliation procedures in modern civil proceedings

Senen Francois Xavier

Conciliation procedures in modern civil proceedings

ScienciaScripts

Imprint

Cover image: www.ingimage.com

This book is a translation from the original published under ISBN 978-620-2-06554-2.

Publisher:
Sciencia Scripts
is a trademark of
Dodo Books Indian Ocean Ltd. and OmniScriptum S.R.L publishing group

120 High Road, East Finchley, London, N2 9ED, United Kingdom
Str. Armeneasca 28/1, office 1, Chisinau MD-2012, Republic of Moldova, Europe
Printed at: see last page
ISBN: 978-620-7-85813-2

Table of contents

Relationship between mediation and arbitration procedures under the new Russian legislation.

In recent years, the issues of alternative ways of dispute resolution cease to be only a subject of doctrinal research and attract special interest of legislators, which is undoubtedly a positive starting point for their introduction and development both in international practice in general and in Russian society in particular. The most attention is paid to the mediation procedure. This is not accidental, as this procedure is recognized as one of the effective ways of conflict resolution in the world.

Unlike arbitration, which in Russia is regulated by different laws depending on the disputes to be resolved (domestic arbitration or international commercial arbitration), the legal regulation of the mediation procedure is based on the Federal Law of 27.07.2010 N 193-FZ "On Alternative Dispute Resolution Procedure with the Participation of a Mediator" (mediation procedure)[1] , the effect of which is as follows

applies to both domestic and international commercial disputes. Thus, in accordance with part 2 of article 1 of the law on mediation, disputes arising in connection with the implementation of entrepreneurial activities and other economic activities are named as disputes covered by the said law. These are the same disputes, which are subject to the jurisdiction of arbitration courts in accordance with part 1 of article 27 of the APC RF. Therefore, the conclusion of E.I. Nosyreva that mediation and arbitration, being independent ways of conflict resolution, can be considered as competing procedures seems reasonable. According to the scientist, when the parties intend to settle their dispute without considering the case on the merits, they choose either mediation or arbitration. And, consequently, the success of one of these procedures usually makes it unnecessary to resort to the others"[2] .

However, as noted by the jurist developing the issue, mediation and arbitration can

1 Sobr. zakonodatelstvo RF. 2010. № 31. Art. 4162. Hereinafter - the Law on Mediation.
2 Davydenko D.L.Commonality between conciliation procedures and arbitration court// Development of mediation in Russia: theory, practice, education: Collection of articles / edited by E.I.Nosyreva, D.G.Filchenko.M.: Infotropic Media, 2012. C.193

"peacefully" coexist, not competing, but on the contrary, complementing each other[3] . This is evidenced by the fact that today organizations with permanent arbitration institutions - courts - offer mediation. In addition, mediation and arbitration can be used sequentially, allowing the parties to diversify the scope of settlement of their dispute. This provision is reflected in the so-called multilevel clause, which is known especially in international practice but is also admissible in national practice. The essence of a tiered clause is that the parties have made a prior commitment to use, for example, mediation to settle a dispute should it arise. However, when the dispute arises, they wish to resort to arbitration. In other words, the parties, or one of them, do not wish to avail themselves of the mediation clause, but simply wish to go to arbitration or to a court to decide the merits of the dispute.

The question arises as to how should a court or arbitral tribunal deal with such a situation? Is arbitration possible if the parties have a mediation clause, or do the parties still have to make use of this clause before going to arbitration? This question is of great practical importance, especially since the law contains a provision that seems to be contradictory.

Thus, the Law on Mediation (Part 1, Article 4) states that if the parties have concluded an agreement on the application of mediation procedure and within the agreed period of time for its implementation have undertaken not to apply to a court or arbitration court for the resolution of a dispute that has arisen or may arise between the parties, the court or arbitration court shall recognize the validity of this obligation until the conditions of this obligation are fulfilled, except for the case when one of the parties needs, in its opinion, to protect its rights. At the same time, part 3 of Article 7 of the said law contains a norm indicating that the existence of an agreement on the application of mediation procedure, as well as the existence of an agreement on the conduct of mediation procedure and the related direct conduct of this procedure, is not an obstacle to appeal to a court or arbitration court, unless otherwise provided for by

3 . Nosyreva E. I. Mediation and international commercial arbitration: possibilities of interaction under Russian legislation / Collection of articles to the 80th anniversary of the International Commercial Arbitration Court at the Chamber of Commerce and Industry of the Russian Federation / Edited by A. A. Kostin. Moscow: Statute, 2012. p. 305

federal law. In this respect, the point of view of E.I. Nosyreva seems to be quite responsive to the question. The author notes that the presence of a mediation clause does not deprive a party of the right to apply to arbitration. At the same time, in her fair opinion, the content of the mediation clause does not matter.[4] In her argumentation, E.I. Nosyreva points out that the peculiarity of a mediation clause is that it can be executed only by both parties: the mediation procedure is based on the voluntariness of the parties and can be initiated only with the consent of both parties.

It seems that such consent is expressed in the conclusion of a mediation agreement, which is the defining moment of the beginning of the mediation procedure. Unlike an agreement to mediate, which is essentially just an anticipation of a dispute resolution option in case of its occurrence, an agreement to mediate is already an expression of the willingness of both parties to initiate the procedure. Thus, it can be said that an agreement on the application of mediation procedure makes sense only in the presence of an agreement to conduct mediation procedure. The latter reflects the mutual agreement of the parties to apply to a mediator to settle their dispute.

As you know, on September 1, 2016 the Federal Law dated 29.12.2015 N 382-FZ "On Arbitration (Arbitration Proceedings) in the Russian Federation" will come into force. This law contains a chapter providing for the correlation of mediation and arbitration procedures (Chapter 10). Part 1 of Article 49 of the Law states that mediation is allowed at any stage of arbitration. However, it does not specify at which stages of arbitration proceedings mediation may be applied.

It seems that the Law on Mediation, which in part 2 of Article 4 provides that if a dispute is referred to a court or arbitration court, the parties may apply the mediation procedure at any time before the decision on the dispute is made by the relevant court or arbitration court. This provision meets the realities and needs of modern society, given that the goal of protecting the rights and legitimate interests of participants in civil turnover is achieved today not only by considering and rendering a decision

---

4 See Nosyreva E. I. Mediation and international commercial arbitration: possibilities of interaction under Russian legislation / Collection of articles to the 80th anniversary of the International Commercial Arbitration Court at the Chamber of Commerce and Industry of the Russian Federation / Edited by A. A. Kostin. Moscow: Statute, 2012. p

binding on the parties, but also by the disputing parties themselves concluding a mutually beneficial agreement. Moreover, the latter method is recognized as the most effective among all means of dispute resolution. The fact is that "if the holder of a certain civil right can freely dispose of it before and outside the process, if he can absolutely refuse it, there is no reason to deprive him of the same free disposal of his rights during the process"[5]

It should be clarified that the application of mediation procedure should not be limited to the moment when the decision is made; it can also be applied after the decision on the case is made by the arbitration court,[6] i.e. at the stage of enforcement proceedings. But at this stage of its application, certain peculiarities should be taken into account, which seem to be due to the special regime of this stage of arbitration proceedings. Indeed, the amicable agreement here is concluded on the dispute already resolved by the court. As such features can be called: firstly, the fact that the submission of the settlement agreement concluded at the stage of enforcement proceedings for approval is made on the basis of the principle of dispositiveness, consisting in the possibility of the parties to apply both to the arbitration court of first instance at the place of execution of the judicial act, and to the arbitration court that adopted the judicial act (part 1 of article 141 of the APC RF). Secondly, when approving a settlement agreement concluded at the stage of enforcement proceedings, the court should not cancel the previously adopted judicial act as it happens when the parties reached a settlement agreement at other stages of appeal, cassation and supervisory review. Here the only and sufficient action of the court is to include in the ruling on approval of the settlement agreement an indication that this judicial act is not subject to execution (paragraph 7, part 7, article 141 of the APC). And, finally, thirdly, the conclusion of a settlement agreement at the stage of enforcement proceedings is admissible in respect of the entire awarded claim and is not allowed to conclude it in respect of a certain part of the claim, as is possible in the case of conclusion of a settlement deal in the process.

5 Vaskovsky E.V. Textbook of Civil Procedure. Ed. 2nd. M., 1917; Textbook on civil procedure. C. 58 - 59.
6 See Resolution of the Presidium of the HAC RF dated June 7, 2012 № 16434/11//Vestnik HAC RF.2012.№ 10.p.312-315.

In our view, the conclusion of a settlement agreement in respect of a part of a claim in enforcement proceedings may complicate the enforcement of the remaining part, since it will require the application of another method of protecting rights. If such a method would be a judicial one, the question arises as to whether it would not be a repeated consideration of the case of the same instance. Thus, it seems that the inadmissibility of concluding a settlement agreement in respect of part of the claims of the lawsuit in the case where the court has already rendered a judgment (at the stage of enforcement proceedings) is quite justified. However, in our opinion, if on the remaining part of the claims the conclusion of any dispositive dispositive action will be reached (the plaintiff's rejection of such claims or their recognition by the defendant), the conclusion of such a settlement agreement should be recognized.

As noted by T.V. Zhukova, the conclusion of a settlement agreement in the process of execution of a judicial act pursues the purpose of refusal of state coercion or termination of compulsory execution, if such a procedure has been initiated[7] . The named author believes that the main reason prompting the parties to enforcement proceedings to conclude a settlement agreement is, unlike in court proceedings, not the disputability of the right, but certain doubts about the possibility to carry out the execution in full[8] . This opinion seems to be correct and corresponds to the present state of affairs.

The significance of the possibility of applying mediation procedures at the stage of enforcement proceedings is also due to the fact that the enforcement of mandatory decisions by the losing party usually causes problems: according to statistics, the level of enforcement of court decisions in courts of general jurisdiction in the country is only 45%. It is not excluded that such problems may also arise in the enforcement of the decision of the arbitration court, since it is as binding as the court decision. Therefore, it is always appropriate and expedient to allow the participants of civil turnover to exercise the right to settle the dispute themselves, as this avoids the problems of non-

---

7 Zhukova T.V. Settlement agreement in enforcement proceedings as realization of the principle of dispositiveness // Arbitration practice. 2005. N 8. C. 83

8 Rozhkova M.A. Basic concepts of arbitration procedural law. M.: Statute, 2003. C. 184.

enforcement of decisions.

In his study of the issue of a settlement agreement in enforcement proceedings, A.H. Ageyev comes to the conclusion that in the case of conclusion of a settlement agreement in the process of enforcement proceedings, the will of its participants (the claimant and the debtor) is given priority over the state-power prescription of the court contained in the court decision[9] . The fact is that by concluding a settlement agreement in enforcement proceedings, the parties acquire the right to change by their will the court decision that has entered into legal force, which even the court itself, which has decided on the case, is not entitled to do (due to the property of immutability of the decision arising from its binding nature), except for expressly provided for cases of supplementing and clarifying the decision and eliminating obvious arithmetical errors. As a rule, such a possibility is an exception to the rule of mandatory execution throughout the territory of the Russian Federation of judicial acts that have entered into legal force.

Another point that requires special attention is the possibility of combining the powers of an arbitrator and a mediator in one person. This issue has been the subject of many years of discussion in the literature. The fact is that mediation and arbitration procedures are different in essence, although they have much in common. Their fundamental difference lies in the functions and powers of the third party. Thus, if, for example, an arbitrator examines the evidence, assesses the validity of the parties' positions in terms of the rules of law and makes a decision binding on the parties, a mediator performs a completely different function. As a rule, his role is to facilitate the convergence of the parties' positions, create favorable conditions for the parties themselves to reach a mutually beneficial solution. The mediator helps the parties to understand each other and, in some cases, to identify various options for the settlement of disputes on terms acceptable to all parties.

In addition, the arbitration procedure is based on the principle of adversarial procedure,

---

9 Ageev A.H. Legal nature of amicable agreement in enforcement proceedings/Arbitration and Civil Process, № 12, 2003 C

while the mediation procedure is conciliatory. Therefore, the issue of the possibility of combining the functions of arbitrator and mediator in one person has a place and is of great practical importance, as it allows the participants of disputable relations to choose the most appropriate method of dispute resolution without violating the essence of each of them, as they function independently.

World practice shows that as a general rule it is impossible to combine the powers of an arbitrator and a mediator. The exception is when the parties mutually agree to authorize the mediator to act as an arbitrator. This provision, for example, is expressly set forth in the UNCITRAL Model Law on International Commercial Conciliation. The law provides that "[u]nless otherwise agreed by the parties, the mediator shall not act as arbitrator in a dispute that was or is the subject of conciliation or in another dispute arising out of the same contract or legal relationship or any related contract or legal relationship". It follows that it is possible to combine the powers of a mediator and an arbitrator in one person only by agreement of the parties.

In addition, combining the powers of mediator and arbitrator in one person is possible within the framework of combined procedures. Combined procedures should be understood as "combining, in different variants, certain features of the main alternative means - negotiation, mediation, arbitration".[10] One of the combined procedures is the procedure called "mediation-arbitration" ("med-arb" for short). The peculiarity of this procedure is that the arbitrator first acts as a mediator between the parties, facilitating the convergence of their positions and their reaching a mutually beneficial solution. Only if the parties fail to reach an agreement, the mediator changes his role and acts as an arbitrator, acquiring the right to make a decision on the dispute binding on the parties. An important condition here is that the parties empower the mediator as an arbitrator.

It is also possible to combine the functions of mediator and arbitrator in one person in such a combined procedure as Arb-mediation, in which an independent third party, acting as arbitrator, makes an award but announces it to the parties only when an

10 Nosyreva E.I.Alternative dispute resolution in the USA.-M., JSC "Publishing House "Gorodets", 2005.-C 123.

attempt to conciliate them as mediator has failed. In essence, the award rendered but not yet announced is not enforceable, but it acquires "the status of a full-fledged arbitral award, enforceable in the general manner existing for arbitral awards after it has been announced to the parties".[11] If the parties have reached an agreement, the earlier award is not announced to the parties and therefore is not enforceable. The advantage of this procedure is that it first of all presupposes agreed solutions, but at the same time it avoids wasting time in case of unsuccessful reconciliation of the parties, since the parties are immediately announced a ready and binding decision.

It should be noted that the procedure of combining several ways- ADR[12] is criticized and is not universally accepted. There is a widespread view that the information that a mediator acquires compromises his position as an arbitrator. It is also believed that giving the powers of an arbitrator to a mediator who has received confidential information from the parties during his separate meetings with each of them, at which the other party was absent, contradicts such a principle of arbitration as the right of each party to hear the position of the other party.[13] However, in our opinion, this is why the issue of combining the functions of a mediator and an arbitrator should be decided by the parties themselves. Moreover, even a person with a conflict of interest may act as an arbitrator, provided that the parties are aware of it but do not object to his/her status as an arbitrator.

The use of mediation in the course of arbitration proceedings also raises a problem related to timing. In accordance with part 4 of Article 49 of the Federal Law "On Arbitration (Arbitration Proceedings) in the Russian Federation", the term of the mediation procedure shall be established by agreement of the parties to the arbitration in accordance with the procedure established by the law on mediation and shall be specified in the ruling of the arbitral tribunal. In this case, the consideration of the dispute shall be postponed for this term. According to the law on mediation (part 3 of Article 13), the term of the mediation procedure shall not exceed one hundred and

11 Davydenko D.L. Correlation of international commercial arbitration with other alternative ways of resolving international commercial disputes / Bulletin of International Commercial Arbitration, 2013, N 1 p 8
12 ADR stands for Alternative Dispute Resolution, from ADR (Alternative Dispute Resolution).
13 Ibid. p. 26

eighty days, except for the term of the mediation procedure after the dispute has been referred to the court or arbitration court, which shall not exceed sixty days. It follows that after referral of the case to the arbitration court, the time limit for mediation is significantly limited and there are no exceptional cases when for any reason it is possible to extend the time limit for mediation. In any case, after the expiry of the prescribed period (sixty days), the mediation procedure shall be terminated and the arbitration proceedings shall continue.

Taking into account that there are exceptional cases for mediation procedures conducted before the dispute is referred to a court or arbitration tribunal, when it is possible to extend the term of the procedure, in particular due to the complexity of the dispute to be resolved, the need to obtain additional information or documents, questions arise as to whether the same difficulties may arise after the dispute is referred to a court or arbitration tribunal.

In our opinion, such an approach does not correspond to the actual state of affairs and puts in a lower position those procedures based on the agreement of the parties, which contradicts the modern world trend of development of procedural law. After all, since the parties to the dispute are in a situation of tension, it may take quite a long time to start the conciliation procedure. After all, the established term may expire before the parties reach the result of the conciliation procedure. Therefore, it would seem appropriate to give judges the discretion to extend the time limit to allow the parties to end the dispute amicably. In order to do so, the court should take into account the degree of likelihood of the parties reaching a positive result. However, in the case of amicable settlement, this will allow to exclude the appeal of the decision, and therefore avoid the burden of the courts of second instance, where the judgment could be appealed.

In this regard, E.I. Nosyreva rightly notes that "even in the case of arbitration courts, including international commercial arbitration, which are more formal than mediation, the terms of proceedings are not established by law. They are provided for by the rules of institutional arbitration or by agreement of the parties"[14] . In the scholar's opinion, the same method should be used in relation to the timing of mediation, regardless of whether it is conducted before or during the arbitration proceedings. Otherwise, setting the term of mediation procedure at sixty days is not in favor of the introduction and development of conciliation procedures, as it may lead to a situation when the procedure is terminated, where the parties have almost achieved positive results, but due to some circumstances need additional time to complete the procedure.

14 Nosyreva E. I. Mediation and international commercial arbitration: possibilities of interaction under Russian legislation / Collection of articles to the 80th anniversary of the International Commercial Arbitration Court at the Chamber of Commerce and Industry of the Russian Federation / Edited by A. A. Kostin. Moscow: Statute, 2012. p

Judicial mediation as an effective tool for the court to realize the task of reconciliation of the parties.

The author of the article considers the issues of application of judicial mediation by the court in the realization of the task of reconciliation of the parties in civil proceedings.

Keywords: Judicial mediation, conciliation, court proceedings, conciliation procedures.

The author of the article discusses questions of application of judicial mediation by the court in the implementation of its task to reconcile parties in civil proceedings.

Keywords: judicial mediation, conciliation, judicial settlement.

In recent years, both abroad and in the Russian Federation, the idea that justice has not only the function of resolving disputes through the absolute application of legal norms, but also a social function, which gives the disputing parties a chance to end the conflict by reconciliation, has become widespread. Plato speaks about this function: "It is necessary that those who have claims against each other, first of all, find their neighbors, friends, and those who know about the actions that constitute the subject of the dispute. Recourse to the court should be undertaken only if a decision properly settling the dispute has not been obtained from these people" <1>.

Voltaire was also convinced of the importance of trying to bring the parties together before going to court. In a letter written in 1739, he congratulated the establishment of peacemakers in Holland, stating: "the best law, the most excellent custom, the most useful I have ever seen in Holland, is that when two people want to sue each other, they must first go to the court of conciliators, called peacemakers" <2>.

According to Paul Ricoeur, justice has two purposes. Its first function is to divide the parties and "give each one what he deserves". And in fulfilling the second function, it achieves the restoration of the social bond. This, according to the philosopher, is the ultimate function of justice<3> . It is the second function that is currently gaining particular popularity, as evidenced by the attention given by researchers, practicing lawyers and legislators to conciliation procedures in democratic and legal states.

Indeed, conciliation as a means of dispute resolution has become a hot topic today. In the context of the current judicial system, which is often considered too slow, expensive, complex, corrupt, biased, dependent, indifferent to the needs of the population, conciliation is emerging as a timely and appropriate response to these shortcomings.

Russian legal literature also substantiates the opinion that the most effective tool for resolving disputes, whether private or even public-law disputes, is their settlement through conciliation procedures. Mediation is one such conciliation procedure, which is recognized as the most effective and widespread, whereby the parties reach a reconciliation with the help of an independent third party. Often, the resolution of disputes through conciliation is prioritized among all the objectives of civil litigation. For example, Nekroshius V. notes that "in the hierarchy of goals of judicial proceedings the leading position is occupied by the goal of reconciliation of the parties, while the resolution of the case on the merits and decision-making should be treated as secondary goals and applied only when it is no longer possible to reconcile the parties" <4>.

A similar approach is followed by T.V. Sakhnova and D.A. Fursov, who assume that ideally the court in civil proceedings "should be interested in finding a "peaceful" resolution of the dispute, in stimulating the parties to such a search"<5>.

B.I. Pospelov also states that "an approach aimed not at judicial resolution of legal disputes and conflicts, but at their peaceful settlement should initially prevail in society" <6>.

In the Reference on the Practice of Application of the Federal Law on Mediation, the Presidium of the Supreme Court of the Russian Federation notes that the development of conciliation procedures is one of the priority areas of improvement of mechanisms for dispute resolution and protection of violated rights of citizens<7>.

It seems that by singling out the reconciliation of the parties as one of the tasks of the stage of preparation of civil cases for trial (Article 148 of the Code of Civil Procedure of the Russian Federation), the legislator also expresses his understanding and sympathy for the procedure of ending the dispute without rendering a binding decision due to its undeniable advantages.

In the conditions of modern democratic society, characterized by complex legal relations that need simplified, fast and cheap settlement, it is necessary to recognize the validity of the approach that recognizes the peaceful settlement of a dispute as the primary goal of civil proceedings, taking into account the essence and foundations of reconciliation and the shortcomings of the modern judicial system, which make this previously the only way to protect the violated and disputed rights and interests of citizens and organizations ineffective.

"Reconciliation of the parties seems to be a desirable way of ending a dispute not only in the interests of the litigants themselves, but also of the State, since the latter is naturally interested in ensuring that there is no strife and disputes between citizens"<8>.

Thus, at present, in addition to resolving the dispute by rendering a judgment, judges are charged by virtue of Article 148 of the Code of Civil Procedure of the Russian Federation with the duty to reconcile the parties. As follows from the content of this article, the task of a judge to reconcile the parties in the course of civil proceedings is limited to the stage of preparation of cases for trial. It seems that such formulation of the task of reconciliation of the parties does not correspond to the actual state of affairs, as it is restrictive, imposing on the court the obligation to promote reconciliation of the parties only at the stage of preparation of the case for trial.

And as it is known, mediation of a dispute already referred to a court or arbitration court for consideration is possible at any time before the decision is made by the relevant court or arbitration court (part 2 of article 4 of the Federal Law on Mediation)<9>. In addition, practice shows the possibility of applying the mediation procedure even after the court decision, i.e. at the stage of enforcement proceedings. Therefore, the task of the court to reconcile the parties should not be limited only to the stage of preparation of cases for trial, but should cover all stages of legal proceedings. This is due to the fact that reaching consensus through mediation, even at the last stage of court proceedings, is always accompanied by great advantages .

First, by achieving a mutually beneficial

Secondly, an agreement reached through mediation offers the parties a chance to maintain further good relations between them, which is of particular importance in personal relationships and economic disputes. Secondly, the reached agreement, as a rule, does not cause difficulties in execution, because the parties who voluntarily entered the procedure, will voluntarily execute its result. This is important especially in modern conditions, when non-execution of court decisions is one of the main problems of the judicial system. It should be noted that according to statistics, the level of execution of court decisions in the country is only 45%<10>. Thirdly, dispute resolution through mediation allows to relieve the courts. The last goal is the center of all initiatives to introduce and develop various conciliation procedures in almost all countries.

The imposition on judges of the obligation to reconcile the parties raises the question of specific actions to be taken by judges at each stage of civil proceedings aimed at reconciliation of the parties. It should be noted that the mediation process itself is not regulated by the CPC, which implies creative work of the court, which is obliged to take the actions specified by law to reconcile the parties.

However, the content of paragraph 5 part 1 of Art. 1 of Article 150(1) of the Code of Civil Procedure of the RF, which discloses the actions of the court aimed at the realization of the task of reconciliation of the parties, is declarative in nature, as it does not specify what measures the court should take to implement this task. According to this norm "the court shall take measures to conclude an amicable agreement between the parties, including the results of the mediation procedure in accordance with the procedure established by federal law, which the parties have the right to conduct at any stage of the proceedings, explain to the parties their right to apply for dispute resolution in the arbitration court and the consequences of such actions".

Resolution of the Plenum of the Supreme Court of the Russian Federation No. 11 of June 24, 2008 "On the Preparation of a Case for Trial" specifies in more detail the actions of the court to reconcile the parties when preparing a case for trial. Thus, paragraph 15 of the Resolution determines that the judge's task is: to explain to the parties the advantages of ending the case in peace; to explain that the legal force of the definition of approval of the settlement agreement is not inferior to the court decision and, if necessary, is also subject to compulsory execution; to explain the consequences of the application of conciliation procedures <11> .

As follows from the meaning of paragraph 5 part 1 of Art. As follows from the meaning of paragraph 5 part 1 of Article 150 of the Code of Civil Procedure of the RF and explained in the Resolution of the Plenum of the Supreme Court of the RF, the actions of the court to reconcile the parties consist only in informing the parties about the advantages and essence of conciliation procedures. There is no doubt that informing the parties about the essence and consequences of conciliation procedures is "an effective tool of propaganda and cultivation of the idea of conciliation in society" <12> and raises no objections, especially at the current stage of their development, when they need special support from both the state and the entire judicial system. However, it should be recognized that one such action is not enough to introduce such an important institution in society. For these procedures to be effective, they cannot be limited to mere explanation; accompanying measures are needed to enable the parties not only to be informed about conciliation procedures, but also to take advantage of them. Otherwise, "in many cases, parties will only be informed about mediation, negotiation, arbitration, but will not actually be able to use them" <13> .

Thus, the judge must take all necessary measures to persuade the parties to make certain concessions and come to an agreement. If the parties are informed of the consequences of ending the case with a judgment and of the advantages of concluding an amicable settlement, they will undoubtedly seek to settle their dispute through conciliation. It is only enough for each party to see its own benefits so that it is willing to go to conciliation with its opponent.

Explanation of the right to settle a dispute with the participation of a mediator presupposes a good understanding of the essence, possibilities and limitations of the mediation procedure<14>. However, based on the fact that the mediation procedure is a new phenomenon in Russian society (at least in its modern understanding), it seems advisable for judges to undergo special training on the essence and techniques of dispute resolution with the help of a mediator. Such training could be organized periodically in the form of advanced training.

It is also possible to organize preliminary meetings of the parties with professional mediators in all courts. The fact is that such mediators with negotiation skills are the most capable of convincing the parties to settle their disputes in peace, as their experience allows them to understand the difficulties often encountered in such a situation, as well as ways to overcome them.

In addition, it is necessary to include such subject as ADR - Alternative Dispute Resolution in the training program of lawyers in various universities in order to prepare the future generation of lawyers - practitioners and researchers with the necessary knowledge in the field of conciliation procedures.

The court's task to reconcile the parties in case the parties use the mediation procedure is also fulfilled by providing them with the necessary time to settle the dispute. In accordance with part 1 of Article 169 of the Code of Civil Procedure of the Russian Federation, the court may postpone the proceedings for a period not exceeding sixty days at the request of both parties if they decide to conduct mediation.

Analyzing the meaning of the above norm, E.I. Nosyreva makes the following conclusions: "the procedural consequence of the application of mediation procedure is only postponement of the trial, but not suspension of the case proceedings or adjournment of the court session; it is also impossible to terminate the case proceedings or leave the application without consideration". Moreover, "postponement of proceedings for the purpose of mediation is a right, not an obligation of the court; if the court has reasons to believe that the mediation procedure may be used solely for the purpose of delaying the process without the intention of the parties to settle the dispute, the court may refuse to postpone the trial" <15>.

In our opinion, postponement of the proceedings should be the duty of the court in any case and it should not be allowed a situation where the parties could have settled the dispute through conciliation (mediation), but due to the fact that the judge did not give them this opportunity, are obliged to fulfill the binding decision made by him. The fact is that even when the parties did not come to an amicable agreement, the very fact of the conciliation procedure does not leave them indifferent.

It should be noted that the established maximum term for postponement of proceedings in a case (within 60 days) cannot be increased either by the court, the parties or the mediator, while the term for out-of-court mediation can be increased by agreement of the parties and with the consent of the mediator up to 180 days. According to V. O. Abolonin, "creation of general terms for all types of mediation and automatic termination of the procedure in case of expiration of the term seems to be a form of excessive and incompetent state interference in private issues of mediation procedure" <16>

The author's observation in this regard seems to be correct and fair, that since the parties to the dispute are in a situation of tension, it may take quite a long time to initiate conciliation proceedings. After all, the time limit may expire before the parties reach the result of the conciliation procedure. Therefore, in our view, it would be advisable to give judges the discretion to extend this time limit to allow the parties to end the dispute amicably. For this purpose, the judge should take into account the degree of likelihood of the parties reaching a positive result. Indeed, the conclusion of an amicable agreement by the parties will avoid a subsequent appeal against the judgment and, consequently, will reduce the workload of the courts of second instance. Of course, the term of the conciliation procedure in a case already submitted to the court cannot be infinite, however, it seems that the term of 60 days without the possibility of its extension does not contribute to the effective implementation of the procedure.

In this case, the experience of France is interesting. According to the current French legislation, the court that accepted the case for proceedings, after obtaining the consent of the parties, appoints a mediator (Article 131-1 of the New Code of Civil Procedure of the Republic of France - NCCP FR) <17> , and determines the terms of mediation. Initially, the initially established terms of mediation may not exceed three months. The mediation period may be extended for the same period at the request of the mediator (Article 131-3 of the French Code of Civil Procedure).

Footnotes

<1> Platon, Les lois, VI p.767

< 2> Nefediev E.A. Selected works on civil procedure// E.A. Nefediev; Lomonosov Moscow State University, Kuban, Kuban.Gos-un-t.-Krasnodar: Soviet Kuban; 2005. M.V.Lomonosov, Kuban, Kuban.Gos-un-t.-Krasnodar: soviet.kuban; 2005. C 325

< 3>. P. Ricoeur, "L'acte de juger", in Le juste, Paris, Esprit, 1995, p. 185-192

< 4> Nekrošius V. Objectives of civil proceedings: establishment of truth or reconciliation of parties? // Russian Yearbook of Civil and Arbitration Procedure. - 2005. - № 4. -SPb. : Izd. dom S.-Peterb. gos. un-ta. 2006. -C.12

< 5> Fursov D.A., Kharlamova I.V. Theory of justice in a brief three-volume presentation on civil cases. Moscow: Statute, 2009. T. 2. C. 410

< 6> B.I.Pospelov.Role of the court in reconciliation of parties in civil proceedings. B.I.Pospelov// Vestnik Omskogo Universitet, "series of law" 2013 c. 2

< 7> Reference on the practice of application of the Federal Law "On alternative procedure of dispute resolution with the participation of a mediator (mediation procedure). Approved by the Presidium of the Supreme Court of the Russian Federation on June 6, 2012 // JPS "ConsultantPlus".

< 8> Nefediev E.A. Selected works on civil procedure// E.A. Nefediev; Lomonosov Moscow State University, Kuban, Kuban.Gos-un-t.-Krasnodar: Soviet Kuban; 2005-2005. M.V.Lomonosov, Kuban, Kuban.Gos-un-t.-Krasnodar: soviet.kuban; 2005.-2005. C 325

< 9> Federal Law of 27.07.2010 N 193-FZ "On alternative procedure for dispute resolution with the participation of a mediator" (mediation procedure)// Collected Legislation of the Russian Federation. 2010. № 31. Art. 4162.

< 10> Khishenko A.S. Conciliation procedures in the process of legal regulation:

historical and legal analysis. Dis.kand.jurid.nauk. Moscow-, 2014. C 77-78

< 11> See: Resolution of the Plenum of the Supreme Court of the Russian Federation from June 24, 2008 N 11 "On the preparation of civil cases for trial" // JPS "ConsultantPlus".

< 12> See B.I. Pospelov. The role of the court in the reconciliation of the parties in civil proceedings. B.I.Pospelov// Vestnik Omskogo Universitet, "series of law" 2013 P. 3

< 13> NaM same. with 4

< 14> Zagainova S.K.Formation in Russia of the practice of mediation in civil cases on the example of the legal experiment "Development and testing of mechanisms for integration of mediation in civil proceedings"//"Herald of Civil Procedure", 2012, N 6 P.9

< 15> See Nosyreva E.I. Application of norms on mediation in civil proceedings // Vestnik of Civil Procedure. 2012. № 6. C 5

< 16> Abolonin V. O. To the question of commercial mediation in Russia // Arbitration and Civil Procedure. 2011. № 4. C. 34.

< 17>. Code de procédure civile français (dernière modification : 25 Août 2016).

Problems of realization of the conciliatory function of the court in the modern civil process.

In recent years, there has been a fundamental change in the understanding of the functions of the court in civil proceedings. In addition to the traditional function of resolving disputes through the absolute application of legal norms, the judge today is also assigned a social function, which consists in his duty to facilitate the settlement of the conflict by the parties themselves on mutually beneficial terms (through conciliation procedures). As rightly notes B.I. Pospelov, "the dialectics of civil procedure brings a new understanding of the role of the court in the resolution of legal disputes, which requires from judges to radically change their views on the process of conciliation, and from the legislator - to prioritize the goals of civil proceedings and further development of conciliation procedures"[15] . Moreover, the social function of the court is very popular and is paid close attention to by the whole legal community. Therefore, conciliation today constitutes one of the duties of the court when considering civil cases, as a result of which it has received legislative regulation in many democratic and legal states.

However, despite all the efforts invested in the development of conciliation procedures and the fact that the merits assigned to them are quite attractive, it should nevertheless be noted that the practical implementation of the conciliation function in the framework of consideration and resolution of legal disputes in Russian courts currently remains ineffective and unsatisfactory. Therefore, the issue of problems and reasons restraining the effective application of conciliation procedures in court remains relevant.

Based on foreign experience, there is reason to believe that one of the problems of realization by the court of its conciliatory function is the incorrect legal regulation of the very obligation of the court to conciliate the parties, which is expressed in a certain contradiction of the norms regulating it. Indeed, by virtue of Art. 148 of the Civil Procedure Code of the Russian Federation (hereinafter CPC RF), conciliation is one of

15 Pospelov B.I.The role of the court in reconciliation of the parties in the civil process. B.I.Pospelov/ Vestnik Omskogo Universitet, "series of law" 2013 c.2 JPS "Consultant Plus".

the five tasks of the stage of preparation of the case for trial. At the same time, part. 5 of Article 150 of the CPC RF enshrines the right of the parties to conduct mediation (conciliation procedure) at any stage of court proceedings.

Foreign experience shows a different approach in the regulation of the court's task of reconciliation of the parties. For example, the Code of Civil Procedure of the Canadian province of Quebec provides that one of the missions of the court considering cases both in first instance and on appeal is to facilitate reconciliation of the parties (part 2 of article 9 of the Code of Civil Procedure of Quebec). A similar approach in the regulation is known to the legislation of the French Republic, where the new Code of Civil Procedure (hereinafter referred to as the Code of Civil Procedure of the French Republic) provides that conciliation is part of the mission of the court when considering and resolving civil cases (Art. 21 of the Code of Civil Procedure of the French Republic). What deserves more attention is that, unlike Russian legislation, the legislation of the French Republic enshrines conciliation as one of the fundamental principles of legal proceedings. Therefore, an attempt to reconcile the parties in French civil proceedings is made at any time and in any place that the judge considers favorable (Art. 129 of the French Code of Civil Procedure).

Such an approach in the regulation of the conciliatory function of the court seems to be reasonable and is more consistent with modern realities and corresponds to the world trend of development of civilization process. In this regard, it is thought that taking such an example in the Russian regulation of the court's task to reconcile the parties would contribute to the development and implementation of such an important institution in the Russian society. Today, no one would argue that, compared to the court's rendering of a decision binding on the parties, the end of a dispute on agreed terms is always accompanied by great advantages and properly meets the real needs of modern society. Under the current judicial system, which itself is slow, complicated, expensive and indifferent to real human needs, conciliation is the appropriate response, which necessitates appropriate regulation.

As a problem of realization by the court of the task of reconciliation of the parties in a case pending before the court can also be highlighted the uncertainty of the range of specific actions of the court, facilitating the reconciliation of the parties. On the pages of the legal press rightly noted the fact that the actions and measures of the court to reconcile the parties, as defined by the legislation of the Russian Federation, are only informational in nature[16] . Nevertheless, given that "the main conciliatory functions in civil proceedings belong to the court, which in some cases is evident even from its name - "justice of the peace""[17] , it becomes obvious that the lack of legislative regulation of specific actions by the judge does not contribute to the effective fulfillment by the court of its duty to conciliate the parties.

Foreign legislative regulation of the main actions of the court to fulfill its conciliation mission in civil proceedings is a vivid evidence of the fact that the development and legislative consolidation of the necessary actions of the court aimed at conciliation of the parties is a necessary condition for the success of conciliation in court. For example, the Code of Civil Procedure of Quebec provides that, in addition to informing the parties, the judge may organize and preside over conciliation meetings at which the parties and mediators must participate (arts. 161 and 162 of the Code of Civil Procedure of Quebec). Such meetings are generally organized to facilitate communication between the parties and to help them understand and assess reality and their own interests and positions, and to consider various solutions that may lead to a mutually acceptable agreement. The participation of mediators in such meetings, in turn, aims at conducting mediation procedures with parties who, after receiving general information about the procedure from the judge, are willing to mediate. This action can play a significant role in reconciliation, because "as long as there is enmity between the parties, no reconciliation is possible; - the destruction of enmity contributes to a sober

---

16 Pospelov B.I.The role of the court in the reconciliation of the parties in civil proceedings. B.I.Pospelov/ Vestnik Omskogo Universitet, "series of law" 2013 c.3 , Bekyasheva D.I. Conciliation proceedings at the stage of case preparation - the future of civil process / World Judge. 2012. No. 6 p. 5, Tsaregorodtseva E.A. Conciliation procedures as a way to optimize civil proceedings// "Publishing House of the Faculty of Law of St. Petersburg State University", 2007 JPS "Consultant Plus", and others

17 Potapenko S.V. Conciliation procedures in the civil process and the role of the court in their implementation: All-Russian scientific-practical conference (December 17, 2014) / North Caucasus branch of the Russian State University of Justice. Krasnodar, 2015published at http://pro-sud- 123.ru/

look at the opponent's claims"[18] .

In France, the civil procedure law provides for the right of the judge hearing cases to initiate conciliation at any stage of civil proceedings (Article 128 of the French Civil Procedure Law). At the same time, judges are given the right to recommend to the parties, at their own discretion, the application of this or that conciliation procedure. Similar experience exists in Norway. According to statistics, when the judge himself applies such an action of conciliation as recommending to the parties a conciliation procedure, the parties agree to it in 50% of cases[19] . Moreover, in certain cases, the French legislation provides for the possibility of conducting conciliation procedures - in particular, the procedure of judicial conciliation[20] by the judge hearing the case or delegating such a mission to a third party (judicial conciliator).

In England, the court's order for the parties to mediate gives rise to what is known as "the disputing parties' duty to consider mediation", the essence of which is to give them a chance to seek the services of a mediator. In this regard, the court has the right to compel the parties to consider the use of mediation, and in order to fulfill this right, the proceedings are suspended. For failure to fulfill the obligation to consider the possibility of mediation, there are sanctions in the form of court costs, which may be imposed if a party knowingly and for objectively unsatisfactory reasons did not properly consider the possibility of mediation[21] .

Thus, in addition to informing the parties, the legislation of the Russian Federation should provide for even greater activation of judges, similar to foreign experience. This can serve as an effective tool for the realization of the task of the court to reconcile the parties, especially since such actions are possible at all stages of civil proceedings and

18 Nefediev E.A. Nefediev E.A. Inclination of the parties to peace in the civil process. Kazan, 1890 *P. 18 - 19*

19Célérité et qualité de la justice. Reports on the experience of Béatrice BLOHORN-BLENNER, Médiatrist of the European Commission, President of the Chamber of the Lyon Court of Appeal, President and Vice-President of the European Group of Magistrates for Médiation (GEMME) p.33.

20 The procedure of judicial conciliation is known in the legislation of France, Canada, Switzerland and Norway. Under conciliation should be understood the procedure of amicable settlement by the parties themselves of the dispute existing between them is based on negotiations with the participation of a third neutral person - the conciliator, or without such a procedure. The procedure of conciliation differs from mediation only in the degree of participation of a third party.

21 The system of civil procedure in England: court proceedings, mediation and arbitration" (Andrews N.)// Translation from English by MIKHAIL Yuryevich Maslov, ed. by R.M. Khodykin "Infotropic Media", 2012 P141-142 SPS "ConsultantPlus".

without affecting the normal course of civil proceedings.

Historical and cultural factors can also be mentioned as a problem in the realization of the conciliation mission in court. The concept of the judge's function in the resolution and consideration of civil proceedings, as the resolution of disputes through the absolute application of legal norms, as well as the application of power by the court to resolve the dispute, always gives priority to the parties. Thus, having applied with a claim to the court for the protection of their rights and legitimate interests, the parties expect it only to make a decision binding on them.

Such a concept is caused by the fact that traditionally the central role of the court is exclusively to consider and resolve the dispute on the merits, from the point of view of the law, while conciliation is carried out by some other persons (conciliators) and outside the court building. Moreover, for a long time and to date, the judicial form of protection of rights and legitimate interests of subjects of legal relations acts as the main, universal and regulated in detail[22] . Therefore, the attempt to reconcile the parties by the judge becomes a surprise and subsequently can rarely lead to positive results. These prejudices constitute a great obstacle to the effective realization by the court of the function of reconciliation in the framework of civil proceedings.

Therefore, it seems that conciliation should be considered not as a secondary function of the judge in civil proceedings, but precisely as its natural and primary function. As B.I. Pospelov notes, "in society, from the very beginning, the approach aimed not at judicial resolution of legal disputes and conflicts, but at their peaceful settlement should prevail"[23] . Also, "the resolution of the case on the merits and decision-making should be treated as secondary goals and applied only when it is no longer possible to reconcile the parties"[24] . At the same time, it is necessary to replace the traditional

22 Reshetnikova O.M. Procedural aspetki application of mediation procedure// Development of mediation in Russia: theory, practice, education: collection of articles / edited by E.I.Nosyreva, D.G.Filchenko.-M.: Infotropic Media; Berlin, 2012.- p.154.

23 Pospelov B.I.The role of the court in reconciliation of parties in civil proceedings. B.I.Pospelov/ Vestnik Omskogo Universitet, "Law Series" 2013 p.2

24 Nekrošius V. Objectives of civil proceedings: establishment of truth or reconciliation of parties? // Russian Yearbook of Civil and Arbitration Procedure. - 2005. - № 4. -SPb. : Izd. dom S.-Peterb. gos. un-ta. 2006. - C.12

concept of the role of the court in the consideration and resolution of civil cases, which consists not only in rendering a binding decision, but also in facilitating the settlement of the conflict by the parties themselves. This, as a rule, is undoubtedly facilitated by enshrining reconciliation as one of the fundamental principles of civil proceedings.

Foreign legislation follows this approach. For example, in the instructions-protocols of the Rules of Civil Procedure

England indicates, for example, that "Courts are increasingly adopting the view that litigation is a last resort and claims should not be brought prematurely when there remains a likelihood of settlement,..."[25] .

Finally, the great congestion that characterizes courts of almost all instances prevents judges from focusing simultaneously on how to resolve disputes on the merits and how to promote conflict resolution by the parties themselves. In such a state of affairs, it seems to us that the judge's greatest concern would be to consider the merits of the case, which leaves no room for reconciliation.

In addition, given that in the performance of all its duties the court must follow a strictly defined procedure and legal deadlines, it becomes difficult for judges to simultaneously realize the objectives of conciliation of the parties, a procedure which by its nature is based on the principle of freedom and flexibility in dispute resolution. In such a case, between a well-described procedure for consideration and resolution of the dispute on the merits and an unregulated conciliation procedure, the judge has a clear choice. Particular attention should be paid to the norm of part 1 of Article 169 of the Code of Civil Procedure of the Russian Federation, which provides that the court may postpone the trial of a case for a period not exceeding sixty days at the request of both parties, in case they decide to conduct a mediation procedure.

Given that the maximum time limit for postponement of the proceedings can never be extended and that the expiry of the time limit would result in a violation of procedural law, the emphasis for the judge is no longer on allowing the parties to resolve their

25 Instruction-Protocols, 4.7

conflict amicably, but on ensuring that there is no violation of procedural law. Such a situation is far from creating favorable conditions for the court to perform its conciliatory function, but on the contrary restrains it.

Therefore, in our opinion, in order to optimize the chances of ending the dispute without a binding decision, it is necessary to create favorable conditions and climate, as it is done in some foreign countries where conciliation is highly practiced. This will avoid the situation when the parties have almost reached a consensus, or there is a high probability to come to an agreement, but due to the expiry of the time limit, they will be obliged to execute a binding judgment issued by the court.

Zarubuzhu legislation gives priority to the peaceful settlement of the dispute. In this regard, the legislation of some countries (e.g. Switzerland) does not even set a time limit for the application of conciliation, thus giving the parties enhanced powers to settle their dispute independently

In other countries (most legislations), there is a maximum time limit for conciliation, but with the possibility of extending it (France, Quebec, Norway, Austria).

In our opinion, in order to avoid abuse of rights by an unfair party, the period of conciliation after the case has been referred to the court should not be indefinite. Therefore, the model of setting a maximum period of conciliation with the possibility of extending it under certain conditions seems to be more acceptable. In addition, the initial period should be reasonable and sufficient. This is because, since the conflicting parties are in a situation of tension, it may take a sufficient amount of time to start the procedure itself.

JUDICIAL CONCILIATION AND MEDIATION AS MECHANISMS OF PEACEFUL DISPUTE RESOLUTION IN MODERN CIVIL PROCEEDINGS: COMMON AND DISTINCTIVE FEATURES

Abstract: The article is devoted to the analysis of judicial conciliation and mediation as alternative mechanisms of protection of rights and interests of citizens in civil proceedings. On the basis of procedural legislations of some foreign countries, their common and distinctive features are studied.

Keywords: Judicial reconciliation, mediation, civil proceedings.

The main priority of a modern democratic society is to improve the existing mechanisms of dispute settlement and protection of violated rights and legitimate interests of participants in civil turnover. To achieve this goal, various measures are taken, one of which is the introduction of various conciliation procedures into the system of mechanisms for the protection of the rights and legitimate interests of citizens. Therefore, today conciliation procedures receive significant development not only outside the courtrooms, but also in front of the judges themselves, sometimes requiring the latter to directly participate in them.

Indeed, while conciliation can be conducted in complete independence from the judicial system (which is in principle in line with the traditional concept of conciliation), parties today are granted

the right to resort to these procedures even when the dispute is already pending in court. In this case, conciliation acts as a tool to mitigate the severity of the legal norm, making it flexible in resolving legal disputes. Thus, today there is a process of expanding the range of procedures for the peaceful settlement of disputes by the parties themselves, which can be applied not only outside of court proceedings, but also within the framework of consideration and resolution of civil cases. As these procedures, judicial mediation and conciliation, considered as the most common and effective ways for the parties to peacefully finalize their differences within the framework of civil proceedings, are of particular importance today.

Russian law and practice today knows mediation procedure as one of the conciliation procedures by means of which the parties can peacefully conclude a dispute after the case has been referred to the court. Moreover, this procedure received legislative regulation with the adoption of the Federal Law "On Alternative Dispute Resolution Procedure with the Participation of a Mediator" (hereinafter - the Law on Mediation)[26] . However, in addition to the mediation procedure, in light of the development of the Concept of a unified Civil Procedure Code of the Russian Federation (hereinafter - the Concept) it is proposed to introduce a new mechanism of dispute resolution within the framework of consideration and resolution of civil cases - judicial conciliation[27] .

Despite the fact that at one time there was a draft law of the Supreme Arbitration Court of the Russian Federation proposing this procedure, judicial conciliation as an independent method of peaceful settlement of disputes remains a novelty for the modern Russian legal system[28] . At the same time, the Concept specifically emphasizes that the procedure of judicial conciliation should not replace the mediation procedure. In this regard, it is of interest to study it in comparison with the mediation procedure. Especially since the differentiation of the two procedures under consideration (conciliation and mediation) in the civilistic process is not always easy.

As already noted, to date, judicial conciliation as an independent procedure for dispute settlement is not known to Russian civil proceedings and practice. Nevertheless, it is widely used in civil proceedings in many foreign countries and has proven to be one of the effective procedures for peaceful settlement of disputes between the parties when the dispute is already pending in court. Therefore, based on foreign experience and taking into account that the Concept does not give a specific answer to the question of differentiation of the two procedures under consideration, it is relevant to identify their

---

26 Federal Law "On Alternative Dispute Resolution Procedure with the participation of a mediator (mediation procedure) from July 27, 2010 N 193-FZ (In editions from 23.07.2013 № 233-FZ, from 02.07.2013 № 185-FZ // Access from the reference. - legal system "Consultant Plus".

27The concept of a unified Civil Procedure Code of the Russian Federation" (approved by the decision of the Committee on Civil, Criminal, Arbitration and Procedural Legislation of the State Duma of the Federal Assembly of the Russian Federation from 08.12.2014 N 124// Access from the reference legal system "Consultant Plus".

28 See: Draft Federal Law of the HAC RF "On Amending Certain Legislative Acts of the Russian Federation in Connection with Improving Conciliation Procedures"// Access from the reference legal system "Consultant Plus".

essence, as well as to highlight their common and distinctive features.

In the literature, the procedures of "judicial conciliation" and "judicial mediation" are often perceived as two identical categories[29] . However, although these dispute resolution mechanisms have much in common, they are at the same time different in many ways. What is common between judicial conciliation and mediation is, first of all, the fact that both are alternatives to traditional judicial protection of rights and legitimate interests of participants in civil turnover. Judicial conciliation and mediation can be used to settle disputes that are already pending in court, and if they are successful, the dispute is terminated and the trial on the merits becomes unnecessary.

Also, mediation and judicial conciliation procedures in civil proceedings are usually carried out on the basis of the principle of voluntariness and with the participation of a third independent person who is not authorized to make a decision binding on the parties. Although the judicial conciliator may propose his or her own version of a solution to the dispute, the latter is not binding until the parties have expressed their agreement with it. In any event, the final decision on the case, whether by judicial conciliation or by mediation, shall be made solely by the parties themselves.

In addition, apart from being voluntary, mediation and judicial conciliation, like all conciliation procedures, are based on the principles of confidentiality, neutrality and impartiality of the third party, cooperation and equality of arms. They are based on negotiation. As a rule, the decision is made by the parties themselves on agreed terms, with maximum consideration of the interests of both parties. The actions of the third party are aimed at facilitating communication between the parties in order to resolve their differences without a binding decision by the court.

The fundamental difference between judicial conciliation and mediation lies in the degree of participation, role and functions of the third party involved. The legislative establishment of the procedure of judicial conciliation abroad shows that the parties themselves can conciliate without the participation of a third party conciliator. In

---

29 See: Bogatina Y.G. Alternative ways of dispute resolution // Arbitration practice. 2006. № 6. C. 24; Primak T.K. Alternative means of conflict resolution // Justice of the Peace. 2010. № 10. C. 10.

France, for example, the new Code of Civil Procedure directly stipulates that the parties may reconcile either on their own initiative or on the initiative of the judge at any stage of civil proceedings (Article 128 of the NGPC FR). Nevertheless, if the participation of a third party in the conciliation procedure may be optional, it has great advantages, since the conciliator contributes to the restoration of the dialog between the parties, thus constituting a necessary and decisive step towards a positive result. Therefore, it seems that for the effective conduct of conciliation in civil proceedings, the participation of a third party should always be recommended.

In contrast to reconciliation, mediation always requires the mandatory participation of a third neutral mediator. The very essence of the term "mediation" (mediation) implies the participation of a mediator between two conflicting persons. In this case, it seems unthinkable to conduct a mediation procedure that would not involve a mediator. Mediation procedure is defined as a method of dispute resolution with the assistance of a mediator on the basis of voluntary consent of the parties in order to reach a mutually acceptable solution (Part 2 Article 2 of the Federal Law on Mediation).

Also, the difference between the procedures of "mediation" and "judicial conciliation" is that the judicial conciliator, as a rule, plays a more active role in the conciliation of the parties than the mediator. The role of the latter is only to organize meetings of the parties, to create favorable conditions for the parties to reach a mutually acceptable solution, without the right to make any decision.

Analysis of the procedural legislation of some foreign countries allows us to conclude that the role of a court conciliator is more active than that of a mediator. For example, in Switzerland, the Code of Civil Procedure enshrines the right of the court conciliator to oblige the parties to appear in person to participate in the conciliation procedure (Article 204 of the Code of Civil Procedure). This legislation also establishes the right of the conciliator to take into account the documents that the parties may submit to him and to conduct an inspection of the scene of the incident. In addition, it stipulates that the conciliator has the right to request other evidence if he is going to propose to the parties his own version of a solution (Art. 203 of the Swiss Code of Civil Procedure).

In France, the new Code of Civil Procedure provides for the possibility for the judicial conciliator, with the consent of the parties, to visit the scene of the accident and to question persons whose testimony is useful to him (Article 129-4 of the Code of Civil Procedure)[30] .

It follows from the above that, unlike a mediator, a judicial conciliator is not limited to facilitating communication between the parties, but also has additional powers (to propose their own version of a solution to the case, to interrogate persons, to conduct an inspection of the scene, to inform the parties about their assessment of the case and the available facts, to give their recommendations or even propose their own version of a solution to the dispute, etc.). In this regard, researchers emphasize that a court conciliator is a particularly active mediator[31] .

As distinctive features of judicial conciliation and mediation, it is also useful to note that *conciliation focuses on facts, whereas mediation focuses on people*[32] . In judicial conciliation, the intention of the parties and their state before the dispute arises and after the dispute is resolved is given less attention than in mediation. In this regard, J. A. Mirimanoff notes that mediation is interested in resolving the conflict, while conciliation aims to reach a solution to the dispute, i.e. the mutual claims of the parties[33] . In other words, conciliation is used where the law can be applied and mediation is used in the rest of the cases[34] . In this regard, the mediator must concern himself with the root causes of the disagreement between the parties; he usually cares about the further development of the personal relationship between the parties. A conciliator, on the contrary, will seek only to overcome the existing differences between the parties, showing no interest in the distant causes affecting them. A judicial conciliator is indifferent to the further relationship between the parties after their conflict has been

---

30 Nouveau Code de procédure civile français (dernière modification : 26 février 2016) https://www.legifrance.gouv.fr

31 Voir: P. KAYSER, "La recherche en France de la diminution des contentieux judiciaire et administratif par le développement des règlements amiables", Justices, 1996, p. 203, spec. p. 208.

32 Voir: Jean A. MIRIMANOFF. Médiation et conciliation : pour en finir avec un psychodrame familial// exposé à la deuxième rencontre des ACBL du 12 Mai 2006 à Grange p. 4 http://www.gemme.ch/rep_fichier/gemme_mediation_et_conciliation.pdf

33 Voir: Thierry GARBY, La gestion des conflits, Economica, Paris , 2004, p.9.

34 Voir: Isabelle Bieri, La justice est-elle une médiation alternative ? Justice and médiation, quelle alternative? Texte de la conférence donnée le 3 octobre 2006 à l'IUKB, p. 5 http://www.gemme.ch/rep_fichier/BIERI_IUK_Justice_et_mediation_20061003.pdf

resolved.

Finally, the difference between judicial conciliation and mediation also lies in the fact that *conciliation develops exclusively within the framework of the law, while mediation is not always subject (at least directly) to the influence of the law.* In this regard, it seems quite fair to note by E.I. Nosyreva and D.G. Filchenko that "judicial conciliation is not a private procedure unlike mediation: it is possible only after the initiation of a case in court, represents a type of judicial activity and is carried out in the courthouse[35] ".

This is why, in our opinion, judicial conciliation is conducted in courtrooms and by persons appointed for this purpose in accordance with the procedure established by law. Also, the fact that judicial conciliation has developed in closer connection with the judicial system than mediation justifies the difference in the requirements for candidates for mediation and judicial conciliation. In particular, in the case of judicial conciliation, higher legal education or experience in the legal field is required along with other professional skills. In this regard, for example, the legislation of some foreign countries (France, Belgium, Switzerland and others) even provides for the possibility of conciliation by the judge himself, who hears cases in the framework of his general mission of reconciliation of the parties. According to the French Decree No. 78-381 of March 20, 1978 "On judicial conciliators", persons with three months of minimum experience in the legal field are appointed as judicial conciliators[36] .

In Russia, according to the Concept, a judicial conciliator may be a retired judge, an assistant judge who does not take part in the consideration of a case, or an employee of the court apparatus who has a higher legal education. It follows that the main requirements for a candidate to perform conciliation activities include the skills of qualification and assessment of available facts, which are associated with legal education. In comparison, this requirement is not known to be imposed on a mediator.

---

35 See: Nosyreva E.I., D.G. Filchenko. Basic provisions of the concept of the institute of reconciliation of the parties in civil proceedings / "Vestnik Civil Process", 2015, N 1// Access from the reference legal system "Consultant Plus".

36 Décret n°78-381 du 20 mars 1978 relatif aux conciliateurs de justice (Version consolidée au 16 février 2017) https://www.legifrance.gouv.fr

In particular, according to the Russian legislation, persons who have reached the age of twenty-five, have a higher education (*not necessarily legal education*) and have received additional professional education on the application of the mediation procedure (part 1 and 3 of Article 16 of the Law on Mediation) may carry out mediation procedures in disputes referred to a court or arbitration court.

Also, judicial conciliation is carried out free of charge for the parties, which means that the state assumes the obligation to reward the conciliator for the service rendered. On the contrary, the mediator carries out his activities for remuneration, which, as a rule, is paid by the parties. In this regard, researchers note that, unlike a mediator, a judicial conciliator acts as a real assistant to the judge in performing his conciliatory function[37]
.

Thus, judicial conciliation and mediation are two different but complementary mechanisms for the peaceful settlement of disputes, which do not exclude each other. With their help, the parties can settle their disagreements without a binding court decision. The introduction of judicial conciliation in Russian civil proceedings makes it possible to diversify the mechanisms of protection of the rights and legitimate interests of civil litigants and gives the parties the opportunity to choose between various conciliation procedures an appropriate procedure that meets their interests. In addition, it seems that judicial conciliation and mediation can be applied sequentially. First, the parties can apply mediation procedure, and if it is unsuccessful, they can resort to judicial conciliation.

37 Voir : Rapp. Magendie, "Célérité et qualité de la justice : les conciliateurs de justice", p. 17.

Classification of conciliation procedures in civil proceedings.

Conciliation procedures can take many forms. This is primarily due to the expansion of the range of conciliation procedures and their constant growth, which can be observed today. At present, for example, there are dozens of conciliation procedures in some countries. The fact is that the conduct of conciliation procedures on principle depends on the will of the parties and is determined by them. Therefore, the authors today offer different criteria for classification of conciliation procedures and there are many difficulties related to the definition of their boundaries. The issue of classification of conciliation procedures has undeniable practical significance, as it allows to distinguish between the existing various conciliation procedures, which in turn contributes to the application to any dispute more adapted procedure for its settlement.

The most generally accepted and basic criterion for classifying conciliation procedures is the scope of their development. All other criteria are usually based on it. This classification criterion is based on the fact that "conciliation procedures as elements of the legal system develop in two directions: within the existing judicial system and outside it"[38] . Based on this criterion, all conciliation procedures are divided into "private" and "public".

1. ***Private conciliation procedures***. These are procedures for the peaceful settlement of disputes, the existence, procedures for conducting and functioning of which are independent of the traditional state judicial system. As a rule, regardless of the type of conflict and by virtue of the principle of dispositiveness that characterizes civil-law legal relations, the parties are always free to organize negotiations and establish the conditions for the conclusion of their dispute without recourse to the court. And if they are unable to conduct such negotiations themselves, the parties may resort to the services of a third party, whose role is to facilitate the settlement of the conflict by themselves. Thus, private conciliation procedures are characterized by "a high degree of disposability with minimal intervention by the State, whose role is only to formally

38 Nosyreva E.I. Alternative dispute resolution in the USA. -M., OJSC "Publishing House "Gorodets", 2005. C 40

recognize them and monitor their legality"[39] .

Conciliation procedures are also characterized by their *implementation in the absence of any connection with the judge or the traditional judicial system.* They are carried out outside of court proceedings: the initiative, the procedure and the execution of the solution reached escape any judicial control. Private conciliation is also known as "extrajudicial conciliation". This category of conciliation is quite broad and can be divided into two subcategories, depending on the degree of formality of their organization. Thus, consensual (ad hoc) and institutional private conciliation procedures can be distinguished.

Consensual conciliation procedures. Procedures for the peaceful settlement of disputes, the implementation, the procedure and the execution of the results of which are not subject to any formalism and are entirely dependent on the will of the conflicting parties. The parties can, for example, freely organize the procedure, set the time and place of its conduct, define the profile of the third party involved in the procedure and its powers, etc.

In some countries (e.g. France), such conciliation may be envisaged from the moment of conclusion of the contract by including a conciliation clause in it, which determines the ways and procedures of dispute settlement in case of their occurrence. In case of application of such procedure, the legislation also provides for the possibility of making the reached agreement enforceable upon application of one of the parties (Art. 1441-14 of the NGPC of the FR). The parties may also, if they wish, apply to a notary, who will confirm their agreement and give it the properties of a notarized act.

Institutionalized conciliation procedures. It is a form of out-of-court conciliation by which a third person (natural or legal), with the necessary training in the peaceful resolution of conflicts, is empowered by the parties or the law, to compare their points of view in order to reach a mutually acceptable solution to the conflict, in accordance

39 Nosyreva E.I. Alternative dispute resolution in the USA. -M., OJSC "Publishing House "Gorodets", 2005. C 40

with the rules organizing this activity[40] .

This category is due to the existence today of various organizations and centers (arbitration centers, for example) offering conciliation services. Abroad and in the Russian Federation, for example, there are dozens of such organizations and centers in different regions. Committing to resort to the services of such organizations, the parties as a rule assume the obligation to obey the initially established rules of internal order, without the right to change them. In their existence and functioning, these organizations have no connection with the judicial system. Therefore, the lack of success of attempts to resolve conflicts within their framework can not affect the right of the parties to apply to the court for the protection of their rights and violated interests. In particular, the failure of this conciliation cannot automatically lead to the consideration of the case on the merits.

In addition to special conciliation centers and organizations, institutional conciliation procedures are carried out in some industries and enterprises that wish to avoid resorting to the state court to settle disputes that arise or may arise between them and their partners.

2. ***Public conciliation procedures.*** Procedures for the peaceful settlement of disputes applied within the framework of civil proceedings. The term "public" conciliation procedures should be understood as those means that are used to resolve conflicts within the court, i.e. on the dispute already submitted to the court and in the course of civil proceedings. Public conciliation is also known as "judicial conciliation". In contrast to private conciliation, public conciliation is conducted in full dependence on the traditional judicial system and involves some involvement of the judge.

Thus, two main characteristics of judicial conciliation procedures can be distinguished: first, they are carried *out within the framework of judicial (civil) proceedings,* and second, they are *conducted under the auspices of a judge.* This requirement necessitates the definition of the criteria for the existence of judicial proceedings,

---

40 Joly-Hurard, Julie. "Chapitre préliminaire. Conciliation et médiation judiciaires, formes de conciliation". Conciliation et médiation judiciaires. By Joly-Hurard. Aix-en-Provence : Presses universitaires d'Aix-Marseille, 2003. (pp. 29-82) Web. <http://books.openedition.org/puam/686>

which in turn helps to determine whether certain conciliation procedures are judicial. Indeed, if the question of the existence of judicial proceedings when the case is referred to a judge for consideration on the merits is not in doubt, the situation may be quite different when the conciliation procedure is carried out in the order of compliance with the claim procedure or on the margins of postponed or suspended proceedings in the case, in cases provided for by law. In these cases, the conciliation procedure can be considered judicial.

In legal literature, civil proceedings (civil procedure) is defined as "regulated by the norms of civil procedural law the activity of the court and other participants in the process to resolve civil cases, verify the legality of court rulings and execution of court decisions[41] ". It seems that the beginning of legal proceedings is associated with the filing of a lawsuit with the court. However, filing a lawsuit in court for protection of rights and legitimate interests is concretized with the initiation of civil proceedings. Therefore, it is the conciliation procedure conducted in the interval of the mentioned period (from the moment of initiation of the case to the execution of the decision) can be considered judicial. In this regard, it seems that the conciliation procedure conducted as a compliance with the requirement of the law can be considered judicial, if it is conducted in the specified period of time.

Also, as we have already noted in the previous paragraph, the legislation of many countries provides for the possibility of postponing or suspending the proceedings in order to give the parties the opportunity to appeal to the conciliator. Given that the outcome of conciliation proceedings has an impact on the fate of the court (termination if the conciliation is successful and renewal or continuation if not), it seems that the postponement or suspension of the proceedings does not deprive the conciliation procedure conducted during the period of postponed or suspended proceedings of its judicial character. Indeed, the postponement or suspension of a judicial instance does not amount to its termination.

In addition, there are situations where the parties, in parallel with the court proceedings

41 V. A. Baranova, Civil Process/// textbook for academic bachelor. vol. 1. Moscow . Yurait . 2015 c.26

in which they continue to appear, conduct negotiations or other conciliation procedures without informing the judge. If they reconciled as a result, such a procedure cannot be considered judicial, as there is no legal connection with the judicial system. In the future, they can perform certain procedural activities: either the plaintiff's rejection of the claim or its recognition by the defendant, as a result of which the proceedings are terminated. It seems that such a procedure has elements of a private conciliation procedure, since the initiative, the procedure and its completion escaped any control of the court.

In addition to the legal connection, a necessary requirement for conciliation to become judicial is that it be *conducted under the auspices of the judge in the* performance of his or her task of conciliating the parties[42] . Regardless of the form of the judge's involvement in the conciliation of the parties (active participation in the search for an amicable solution or control over a third party conciliator), such intervention by the judge always acts as an instrument for the realization of his conciliatory function.

In addition to private and public conciliation procedures, there are also conciliation procedures, which have elements of private and public conciliation procedures. In foreign legal literature, such procedures are referred to as *"conciliation para-judiciaire" (French: "conciliation para-judiciaire", literally "para-judicial conciliation procedures").* The main characteristic of these procedures is that, while they are conducted by independent third parties and outside any court of law, they nevertheless maintain a narrower connection with the judge. This connection may, for example, be manifested in the procedure for appointing a conciliator, or in the mechanisms for organizing the procedure itself, or in the possibility of appealing to a judge. In addition, another element that characterizes a para-judicial conciliation procedure and brings it closer to a private one is its autonomy in relation to any judicial proceedings. Such procedures include institutional conciliation procedures, which are derived from a law or decrees[43] . In France, for example, there is Law No. 84-148 of

42 Joly-Hurard, J. 2003. Chapitre préliminaire. Conciliation et médiation judiciaires, formes de conciliation. In Conciliation et médiation judiciaires. Presses universitaires d'Aix-Marseille. doi :10.4000/books.puam.686

43 Joly-Hurard, J. 2003. Chapitre préliminaire. Conciliation et médiation judiciaires, formes de conciliation. In Conciliation et médiation judiciaires. Presses universitaires d'Aix-Marseille. doi :10.4000/books.puam.686

December 1, 1984, on the settlement of disputes related to the difficulties of enterprises, as well as Law No. 89-1010 of December 31, 1990, which establishes a procedure for the peaceful settlement of disputes related to insolvent persons.

Although the existence and conduct of the procedure has a close connection with the judicial system, it should be conducted outside of court proceedings so that its failure or success does not affect the normal course of the proceedings. As a rule, after the failure of this conciliation procedure, the parties retain the right to appeal to the court for consideration of the merits of the case. This procedure has the advantage of defining a new form of conciliation that does not belong to one of the two traditional forms of conciliation.

Thus, para-judicial conciliation is a form of conciliation that involves a third neutral person and takes place outside of court proceedings, but in close connection with the judicial system. The intervention of the judge is not directly concerned with the procedure itself, but with its organization. As a rule, the involvement of the court is at the request of the parties or the conciliation organization.

In the legal literature there are different criteria for classification of conciliation procedures. Of interest is the opinion of Kolyasnikova Y.S., who in the basis of division of conciliation procedures puts the stages of possible conflict resolution, at which the parties turn to a particular procedure. In this regard, the author distinguishes five groups of conciliation procedures at[44] : pre-trial; extrajudicial; judicial; post-trial; and conciliation procedures applied in enforcement proceedings.

1. *Pre-trial conciliation procedures.* They are used by the parties only before applying to a state court to protect their rights and interests and are independent of the state court system.

2. *Out-of-court conciliation procedures.* These procedures are used after going to court, but with the aim of settling the dispute amicably without a court decision and require procedural actions on the part of the court, such as suspension of proceedings.

---

44 KOLYASNIKOVA Y. S. conciliation procedures in the arbitration process / Abstract of Cand.jurid.nauk. Ekaterinburg, 2009 P 18

3. *Judicial conciliation procedures.* These procedures are used after going to court and before a judgment is rendered, and the third party facilitator is the court.

4. *Post-judicial conciliation procedures.* The dispute settlement procedures of this group are effective after the dispute has been considered in court and a writ of execution has been issued, but before enforcement proceedings have been initiated.

5. *Conciliation procedures used in enforcement proceedings.* Using such procedures, such as a settlement agreement, the parties can agree on the order and terms of execution of a judicial act.

One can agree with the author, but it should be noted that some points in her proposed classification are controversial. In particular, speaking about out-of-court conciliation procedures, the author notes that they differ from pre-trial procedures in that the procedure for resorting to them requires certain procedural actions of the court (announcement of a break in the court session, postponement of the trial, suspension of proceedings).

However, as already noted, postponing or suspending proceedings in a case does not terminate the judicial instance, which continues to exist. In other words, the conduct of conciliation during a postponed trial does not mean that the procedure is conducted outside the trial for several reasons: first, the trial still exists and the procedure is conducted within it. Secondly, even when the said procedure is conducted by a third party, it remains closely linked to the judicial system and is subject to certain peremptory norms. For example, the maximum period of time for the said procedures and the status of the third party are determined by law. Thus, we consider it unreasonable to consider as extrajudicial, the procedure conducted during the postponed or suspended court proceedings. In our opinion, such a procedure meets all the conditions of judicial conciliation.

In addition, as correctly notes M.S. Nakhov "judicial procedures, as well as out-of-court procedures, are quite permissible after appealing to the court" and in both cases the procedures require certain procedural actions on the part of the court[45] ". This allows us to conclude that extrajudicial conciliation procedures as defined by Kolyasnikova Y.S. coincide with judicial conciliation procedures.

Also, it is thought that the category of extrajudicial conciliation procedures should cover all conciliation procedures conducted before filing a lawsuit with the court, as well as after the court decision. In other words, post-judicial conciliation procedures, judicial conciliation procedures conducted in enforcement proceedings should constitute the category of "extrajudicial conciliation procedures". The above mentioned conciliation procedures as a rule do not depend on the state judicial system and do not require certain procedural actions by the court.

According to T.V. Chernishova, the following classifications of conciliation procedures can be distinguished: pre-trial (out-of-court) conciliation procedures; judicial conciliation procedures; universal conciliation procedures[46] .

- *Pre-trial (extrajudicial) conciliation procedures* are methods used by the participants of the disputable legal relationship to settle the existing differences between them, before resorting to the court. In the author's opinion, for the application of these methods, the participation of the court is not assumed and the active role is given to the parties to the disputes themselves. The role of the court may consist only in fixing and verifying the fact of committing the procedures when accepting the statement of claim, if the contract or the law provides for a mandatory claim or other pre-trial dispute resolution procedure.

- *Judicial conciliation procedures are* used by participants in civil proceedings in order to "peacefully" resolve a dispute directly in court. The fact that judicial conciliation procedures are applied in court explains why they are carried out under the control of the court or with its direct participation. In addition, "in certain cases, they have binding legal consequences, as the court may give the conciliation procedure,

45 Nakhov M. S. Mediation as a mechanism for realizing the purpose of civil proceedings / Cand.jurid.nauk. Saratov, 2014 P. 94-95

46 Chernyshova T.V. The concept and types of reconciliation in Russian law// Journal of Russian Law. 2010. № 12. "JPS Consultant Plus".

formalized in the form prescribed by law, an authoritative and binding character".

- *Universal conciliation procedures are* used by the parties to legal conflicts to settle disputes that have arisen between them, throughout their dynamics (before bringing a claim to court or even after such a claim, i.e. within the framework of civil proceedings). To this group the author refers amicable agreement, mediation and negotiation.

According to the criterion of participation of a third party in them, it is possible to distinguish conciliation procedures, which are conducted by the parties themselves without the participation of a third party; and conciliation procedures, in which a third party participates. The conciliation procedures of the first group include negotiations (a method of peaceful settlement of disputes conducted by the parties themselves, by means of harmonizing their interests in order to reach a mutually acceptable solution to the dispute). These procedures are known to the legislation of practically all states. Indeed, negotiations form the basis of all other conciliation procedures, which are only their "variations, complications and improvements"[47] .

Mediation, conciliation, amicable agreement can be referred to conciliation procedures conducted with the participation of a third party. The third party involved in conciliation procedures is not a party to the dispute as only the parties are. His role is to organize negotiations between the parties, to create favorable conditions for them to conclude an amicable agreement. Despite the fact that the third person may be authorized to make a decision in certain cases, it is not binding on the parties until they have expressed their consent to it.

It seems that conciliation procedures can be classified depending on whose initiative they are conducted. According to this criterion, we can distinguish between conciliation procedures initiated by the court and conciliation procedures initiated by the parties themselves.

The laws of many States provide for both options for initiating conciliation. The more

47 Davydenko, D.L. Mediation as a conciliation procedure in commercial disputes: essence, principles, applicability / D.L. Davydenko // Business and Law. - M., 2005. - № 5. - C. 123

common option is that of conciliation initiated by the parties. Indeed, all conciliation procedures are based on the principle of voluntariness, which is usually expressed in the initiation of conciliation. Nevertheless, the laws of some countries derogate from this rule and provide for the option of initiating the conciliation procedure by other persons, in particular by a judge.

In England, for example, a judge has the power to recommend that the parties suddenly resort to mediation, which gives rise to a "duty to consider mediation. Sanctions may be imposed on a party who fails to do so. In France, the procedural legislation provides for the possibility of reconciliation of the parties on their own initiative or on the initiative of the court at all stages of civil proceedings (Article 128 of the NGPC FR). Such a variant of conciliation procedure is also known in the legislation of Belgium. Taking into account the current legislation, it should be noted that the Russian Federation is characterized only by conciliation procedures conducted solely on the initiative of the parties.

Depending on the degree of court involvement and its authority, all conciliation procedures in civil proceedings can be divided into conciliation procedures with a classical conciliation system; conciliation procedures with a mediating role of the judge; alternative judicial conciliation; conciliation procedures with subsequent judicial control[48] .

Conciliation procedures with a classical conciliation system involve minimal court involvement. Its role is as follows: to explain to the parties their rights to conclude a settlement agreement and the consequences of their exercise; to create favorable conditions for the parties to reach a mutually acceptable agreement; to control the compliance of the reached decision with the law; to formalize the reached agreement; and to assist in enforcing the settlement agreement in case one of the parties refuses to voluntarily execute it. This type of conciliation is characteristic in most states (including Russia) and is fixed in the procedural legislation. For example, the Civil

48 ZDROK O.N. Conciliation procedures in civil proceedings:concept, classification, tendencies of development (on the example of the Republic of Belarus)/ "Vestnik Civil Process", 2010, № 1 "Consultant Plus" JSS Consultant Plus

Procedural Code of the RF enshrines the duty of the judge to facilitate conciliation of the parties and the possibility for the parties to conclude an amicable agreement at all stages of civil proceedings (Article 148, Part 5, Article 150 of the Civil Procedural Code of the RF). This variant of conciliation procedure is in force in the Republic of Belarus (Article 285 of the CPC), in Poland (Article 223 of the CPC), in France (Articles 127-129 of the NGPC), and in other[49] .

Conciliation procedures with the mediatory role of the judge presuppose the active participation of the judge who accepted the case for consideration. In these procedures, the judge acts as conciliator, with the right to hear the dispute on the merits if the parties fail to reach a positive result. In Belgium, for example, the procedural law provides that an attempt at conciliation is made by the judge who hears the case on the merits if the conciliation procedure is not successful (Art. 1344). This type of conciliation procedure is also applied in China, Vietnam and the Netherlands.

A disadvantage of this conciliation procedure may be that it combines the powers of judge and conciliator in one person. This may compromise the principle of confidentiality that characterizes conciliation. In addition, in some cases, "judges, balancing their judicial and mediation roles, often actively use the threat of judgment in negotiations[50] ".

That is why, today, a variant of conciliation procedure with the mediating role of the court is becoming widespread, where the judge who performs the role of mediator loses the right to consider the case on the merits in case of failure of the procedure. Such experience is also known in the legislation of Canada and Norway, where, in order to ensure the principle of confidentiality, it is provided that in case of failure of the conciliation procedure conducted by the judge, the case is transferred to another judge for consideration in the ordinary judicial order[51] .

Alternative judicial conciliation is a dispute resolution procedure involving the

49 Zdrok. O.N. Conciliation procedures in civil proceedings:concept, classification, tendencies of development (on the example of the Republic of Belarus)/ "Vestnik of civil procedure", 2010, No. 1 "Consultant Plus".
50 See ibid.
51 JEAN A. MIRIMANOFF. Mort ou renaissance de la conciliation judiciaire en suisse. RDS, I, No 5, 2004, P.554-555.

separation of the functions of the court to hear the case and conciliate the parties[52] . This variant of conciliation procedure assumes the performance by the court, in addition to the traditional function of administration of justice, of a mediatory function within the framework of a separate type of proceedings. This type of conciliation procedure may include such type of conciliation, which is known to the French legislation and consists in the possibility of the parties to apply to the court with a request for a preliminary attempt of conciliation (Article 830 of the NGPC FR). In this regard, the judge is obliged to carry out the conciliation procedure either by himself or to delegate this mission to another person. This conciliation procedure is carried out in the course of an independent type of proceedings, in which the parties must appear in person. This conciliation procedure is an independent type of legal proceeding, which consists in calling the opposing party to conciliation through the court.

According to Articles 184 - 186 of the Polish Code of Civil Procedure, the court is obliged to seek conciliation even before the commencement of the proceedings. For this purpose, the court may conduct conciliation proceedings prior to the initiation of proceedings on the claim of the interested party. The application for initiation of conciliation proceedings is made without regard to the rules of subject matter jurisdiction to the district court at the place of residence of the opposing party. The conciliation procedure shall be conducted by a judge alone in a court session, the course and results of which shall be recorded in the minutes. The amicable agreement, if concluded, shall be signed by the parties and attached to the minutes[53] .

Conciliation procedures with subsequent judicial control are dispute resolution procedures carried out by a third party whose activities remain under the full control of the court. In France, the legislation provides for the possibility for the court to delegate the mission of conciliation of the parties to a third party (Art. 192-2 CPC FR). For this purpose, the judge appoints a judicial conciliator and sets the term of the procedure. The court conciliator shall inform the judge about all the difficulties he/she

52 Zdrok. O.N. Conciliation procedures in civil proceedings:concept, classification, tendencies of development (on the example of the Republic of Belarus)/ "Vestnik of civil procedure", 2010, No. 1 "Consultant Plus".
53 Zdrok. O.N. Conciliation procedures in civil proceedings:concept, classification, tendencies of development (on the example of the Republic of Belarus)/ "Vestnik of civil procedure", 2010, No. 1 "Consultant Plus".

encounters in performing his/her conciliation function, as well as about the success or failure of the conciliation. The judge may terminate the conciliation procedure at any point, at the request of one party or at the initiative of the conciliator. He may also automatically terminate the conciliation procedure if, in his opinion, its positive outcome is compromised (Art. 129-5 of the Civil Procedure Code).

Depending on the mandatory application of the procedures, it is possible to distinguish mandatory and voluntary conciliation procedures. *Mandatory conciliation procedures are* understood as procedures for the peaceful settlement of disputes, without the prior conduct of which the claim of the interested party to the court is not accepted. This procedure exists in Argentina, where the Argentine Law of October 25, 1995 on Mediation and Agreement makes judicial mediation mandatory for most disputes. The mediation procedure is conducted with the mandatory presence of the parties. A party who fails to appear may be sanctioned with a fine. The settlement agreement reached in the mediation process is signed by the mediator, the parties and their lawyers and is enforced in court as a court decision. In case the amicable agreement is not reached, the parties are issued a document authorizing them to submit the claim to the court for consideration on its merits (Articles 12, 14).

Based on the principle of voluntariness that characterizes all conciliation procedures, it can be said that all conciliation procedures are generally optional. Compulsory conciliation procedures in this regard constitute something of an exception.

Depending on the number of parties involved, conciliation procedures may be *bilateral* and *multilateral*. По категориям дела или видам споров можно выделить *примирительные процедуры по спорам из частноправовых* или *публично-правовых отношений*, *примирение в процессе рассмотрения гражданского дела судом общей юрисдикции* или *арбитражным судом* либо *в процессе исполнения решения*, *примирительные процедуры в международном праве*, *примирение сторон международных и внутригосударственных споров*; *примирение сторон внутренних (внутрикорпоративных)* и *внешних конфликтов*; *разрешение конфликтов только между частными лицами*, только *между публичными лицами,* разрешен

According to the nature of participants, conciliation procedures may be divided into conciliation procedures between individuals or legal entities, conciliation procedures with the participation of state and municipal bodies.

Depending on the instance in which the dispute is considered: conciliation procedures applied in the course of consideration of the case by the court of first instance, and conciliation procedures applied in the course of consideration of the case by the court of appeal.

The criterion for classifying conciliation procedures may also be the participation of a third party. In this case, it is possible to distinguish conciliation procedures conducted by the parties themselves without the participation of a third party, and conciliation procedures in which a third neutral person participates. The conciliation procedures of the first group include negotiation and amicable settlement. Mediation and conciliation are examples of conciliation procedures involving a third party.

Conciliation procedures can also be ranked according to the status of the entity conducting them. According to this criterion, we can distinguish between conciliation procedures conducted by the parties themselves; conciliation procedures conducted by a judge; and conciliation procedures conducted by a mediator or conciliator. As a rule, conciliation procedures are carried out by the parties themselves, as they are the ones who primarily benefit from the settlement of the dispute. Therefore, conciliation procedures may be carried out by them themselves. The involvement of a third party is intended to address the emotional tension that the parties are under at the beginning of the dispute, which makes it difficult for them to cooperate in the settlement of the dispute.

Thus, a judge may act as a third party facilitating conciliation. This type of conciliation procedure is known abroad, for example, in France, Canada, China, Switzerland, the USA, and other countries where the procedure of conciliation (conciliation) is applied. Russian legislation and practice are familiar with conciliation procedures with the participation of a mediator, whose status is determined by the Federal Law.

MIX
Papier aus verantwortungsvollen Quellen
Paper from responsible sources
FSC® C105338

Printed by Books on Demand GmbH, Norderstedt / Germany